SPECIAL FORCES

John Fisher

BROADWAY PLAY PUBLISHING INC
224 E 62nd St, NY, NY 10065
www.broadwayplaypub.com
info@broadwayplaypub.com

First printing: November 2012
I S B N: 978-0-88145-542-7

Book design: Marie Donovan
Page make-up: Adobe Indesign
Typeface: Palatino
Printed and bound in the U S A

SPECIAL FORCES was first presented by Theater
Rhinoceros in May 2007. The cast and creative
contributors for this production were as follows:

COLONEL	John Fisher
DAME	Sage Howard
HAZLITT	Elias Escobebo
BRAVER	William J Brown, III
SOMERS	A K Conrad
BLUE	Matthew Martin

Director	John Fisher
Composer	Eric DeLora
Accompanist	Tom Shaw
Sound design	Tanner Mennard
Scenic design	Mark Paisly
Lighting design	Dave Robertson
Stage manager	Sarah Chase
Photography	Kent Taylor

CHARACTERS & SETTING

COLONEL GERALD JESSUP, U S M C: *mid-forties, fit*

LIEUTENANT "DAME" ANDERSON, U S M C: *female, late-twenties, very fit*

LIEUTENANT THOMAS HAZLITT, U S M C: *(pronounced Haze-lit) late-twenties, handsome*

SERGEANT BILL BRAVER, U S M C: *early-twenties, a professional*

SERGEANT JAKE SOMERS, U S M C: *twenties, a little green*

DINAH BLUE: *male, indeterminate age, relaxed, seen it all, a male actress (but, as he'll insist, not a drag queen)*

Scene: Kuwait City; Northern Iraq

Time: 2003

Situation: Operation Iraqi Freedom

PRODUCTION NOTE

SPECIAL FORCES is performed without intermission on a bare stage that comes to represent all the locales depicted. Some visible columns (as many theaters have in the middle or periphery of their stage) and a fire door visible upstage (as many theaters have if you build no set) are helpful. A curtained area running along the right side of the audience area is also helpful. "Shift" in the script can be achieved with lights, turntables or simply a shift in focus from one side of the stage to another. Furniture for various scenes can be preset on the perimeter and brough into place when needed. Actors in different locations can occupy the same playing area.

for Michael

Scene 1

(March, 2003. A U S Marine Corps base outside Kuwait City. The COLONEL *speaks to his men, which is not what bird colonels usually do. Being an officer and therefore a snob, he should only talk to his officers. But the* COLONEL, *as is evident, likes talking to his men; he is John Wayne—or Jean-Claude Van Dam—in his own little war movie, he writes the script, he directs the actors, he sets up the shot. He is their* COLONEL.*)*

COLONEL: *(To the audience, as if they were his men)* As some of you know this is meant to be a cheap war. Bush Père did with two million men and six months of war what we're going to do with forty thousand and one month. There will be fewer casualties, fewer repercussions, and less shit from the press. When we leave we'll leave behind a country free from tyranny and an economy more closely aligned with American interests. If that sounds optimistic and cynical to you remember, we're in the business of staying in business—both as Americans and as Marines. The last war almost destroyed the military it was such a fuckin' mess, this one will be efficient and effective. When we're through, Americans at home will see we can function like any other industry be it high tech, entertainment, or finance: we cut costs, increase revenue and bring results.

MEN: Arrugah!

(The men are of course scattered throughout the audience, as men are in plays like this.)

COLONEL: *(Referring to a map)* You'll be dropping into Northern Iraq. As you know, up there it's all about bridges. The Kurds have them, the Republican Guard want them, we're going to hold them. We have friends on the ground. So long as we're friendly. Don't go shooting at everything that shits. Remember your R O E. You have enough firepower and protection to let the other guy fire first. But when they fire, you blow they're fucking heads off. First Squad, Tiger Tiger Tango, your objective: The Hussein Highway Bridge across the Tigris at Bikrit. You'll debark at 0300 on the day of, hit the bridge at 0530, turn it over to our Kurdish contacts at 0700 and move on to our next objective. Now—

HAZLITT: *(From a seat in the audience)* Sir.

COLONEL: Yes, Lieutenant.

*(*HAZLITT *is everything we expect: the next John Wayne. He is young, attractive, tall with the sheen of blond hair highlighting a curvaceous trim torso, a god. The* COLONEL *would be jealous of him, of his youth, if he wasn't so much in awe of him and the fact that* HAZLITT *is his soldier, his chick. The* COLONEL *sat on this egg, hatched it and now beams at his own creation.)*

HAZLITT: What is our next objective?

COLONEL: *(Smuggly)* Ladies and Gentlemen, Lieutenant Tom Hazlitt.

(A raucous cheer from the men—obviously HAZLITT *is a popular officer.)*

COLONEL: You'll learn about that when you've secured the bridge.

HAZLITT: But when do we ignite, sir?

COLONEL: That's up to Baby Bush. Be seated.

(The COLONEL, *like Ulysses S Grant before him, has an inherent distrust of passing on information to anyone before it is necessary for them to know it. For all his vanity, the* COLONEL *knows that briefings can turn quickly into brag sessions, the master planner giving away too many secrets he's so impressed with his own acumen. Everything leaks, even the vessel you trust the most. The* COLONEL's *rebuke to* HAZLITT *is gentle and reassuring, he's confident that his men understand his reticence.)*

HAZLITT: Yes, sir.

COLONEL: *(Summing up)* I remind you: you are trained professionals. Like brain surgeons, torch song singers, and Thai prostitutes. This isn't about John Wayne or the Junior League. Don't go bein' heroes or saints. Stick to plan, do your job, and let's all get home safe. The name of the game is success and every Goddamn one of you comes home in one piece. Capiche?

MEN: Capsico!

COLONEL: Lock and load!

MEN: Get some!

Scene 2

(Lights change. COLONEL *is folding up his laptop talking to* DAME. *She's the real thing—Corps, Corps, Corps, right down the line. She's seen the commercials, loved the life and now she's living it. When she was little she never dreamed a woman could get this far, actually prepping for a combat jump and being taken seriously by a bird colonel. But here she is. She greets the moment with the calm and coolness of the true enthusiast. She also knows she's part of a team and a team is all about appearances. She's not going to lose her main chance because of a member of her team. The* COLONEL

*is all business with her. He likes that about her, he doesn't
need to be chummy.)*

COLONEL: I don't want to hear a lot of bullshit about
this mission.

DAME: No, sir.

COLONEL: It's a simple grab and ice op. Go north,
grab the bridge or smoke it and move on to your next
objective.

DAME: Which is?

COLONEL: Hazlitt will know.

DAME: *(Fishing)* The ice?

COLONEL: *(Not biting)* Hazlitt will know. You're both
in charge. He's brains, you're brawn. He'll know the
objectives.

DAME: 10-4, sir.

COLONEL: *(Turning on her, talking to her as a woman)*
And whatever happens, Dame, don't you, don't *you,*
get caught.

DAME: I understand, sir.

COLONEL: Simple operation.

DAME: Simple as pie, sir.

COLONEL: Piece a cake.

DAME: *(Relaxing into specifics)* I'm in touch with
A A I and we should have some word by morning
about transport. It'd sure be nice to swing this one
without a drop.

COLONEL: Yeah, it would. That depends on the Turks.
We're not too pop with Ankara right now.

DAME: Has Hazlitt actually ever jumped? Combat
jumped.

COLONEL: Don't worry about Hazlitt. He's a good kid.

DAME: If he hasn't jumped there's a greater likelihood of him breaking—

COLONEL: He'll be fine.

DAME: I'm concerned, sir.

COLONEL: *(Wheeling on her, not angry, just definite)* You're my fair-haired girl, Dame. Ya know that?

DAME: Yes, sir.

COLONEL: Hazlitt's my fair-haired boy. Same prejudice that protects you, protects him.

DAME: Yes, sir.

COLONEL: You're my team. You're not perfect but you're mine. We wait around for the *right* team, Colonel Weiss or Colonel Rodriguez will beat us to the punch. They got teams too. They just don't got the jump. I did the research, I went to the general, I convinced him, I got the go. We're going. Green light.

DAME: Yes, sir.

COLONEL: Hazlitt's not jumped in combat, you're not a boy. I overlook both deficiencies.

DAME: Yes, sir.

COLONEL: Hazlitt's jumping.

DAME: Yes, sir.

(Pause. COLONEL and DAME regard one another.)

DAME: Thank you sir.

COLONEL: *(Back on track)* Where is he?

DAME: *(Good natured)* A-WOL in K C.

COLONEL: But where?

DAME: Don't know sir.

COLONEL: Can you find him?

DAME: Yes, sir.

COLONEL: Quickly?

DAME: Sir.

COLONEL: *(Suddenly different, worried)* So where is he?

DAME: Don't ask, don't tell sir.

COLONEL: *(More annoyed than suspicious)* What the hell are you talking about?

DAME: Are you serious, sir?

COLONEL: Where is he?

DAME: In K C, sir. He's on leave.

COLONEL: Where is he? Some whorehouse?

DAME: I know where he is, sir.

COLONEL: I want you to be able to find him.

DAME: Yes, sir.

(Pause)

COLONEL: Where is he?

(Pause)

DAME: Blue Parrot.

COLONEL: What's that?

DAME: Skank hole, sir.

COLONEL: Skank hole?

DAME: Other side of the river.

COLONEL: You know where he is.

DAME: Absolutely sir.

COLONEL: So long as you know.

DAME: Yes, sir.

(Blackout)

Scene 3

(Music is heard. Spot up on DINAH BLUE *in the Blue Parrot, Kuwait City. She is everything we expect from the publicity—fabulous, but very real. Though a man in a dress and other accoutrements, she is not a drag queen, as we shall see. She is something more, or different. The point is, she's* DINAH BLUE *and any further introduction would only diminish the reality. [A difficult part to cast: she must be a performer with experience in this trade. Experience, beauty, and a sense of centrality. Whatever the realities of the narrative, she must play this play as if it were about her, as is everything in her life.] She is dressed in blue, always. She sings; using the front row of patrons as if they were patrons at the club. To the side of the audience is a small table—part of the permanent audience set-up. Audience members may sit at this table, but one seat remains empty for these scenes in the club. In this scene,* HAZLITT *sits at the table.)*

(Song: Kuwait City*)*

BLUE: *(Sings)*
Kuwait City, how I love ya
All the sheiks here, squeaky clean.
But the ladies you can't see 'em.
Could they all be chic drag queens?

I go shopping in my shador
Get the bargains and respect.
Show some leg here, you're a whore here.
It's much worse than you expect.

When you travel in the wake of
The Marine Corps, the Navy

You're an expert at decorum
All those gentlemen, you're the lady.

So where next year? Perhaps Beirut?
Samarkand, kid? Bukhara?

Maybe Georgie has his sites on
Guatamala. North Korea?

I get nervous watching T V.
9/11, Afghanistan.
All those weapons—mass destruction.
I'm just here boys, to get a tan.

Kuwait city, how I love ya
All the sheiks here, squeaky clean.
Oh, the war here is so hot here
Makes the men here freaky mean!

(The number ends. Blackout. Applause as we…)

Scene 4

(Shift to BLUE's *dressing room backstage at the Blue Parrot. There is a vanity, chair and screen. On the screen, posters of* BLUE's *appearances around the world. She obviously has quite a track record in Third World hot spots.* BLUE *is discovered removing her make-up. A knock is heard. A specific knock: knock, knock, knock [pause] knock.* BLUE *smiles.)*

BLUE: Come in.

*(*HAZLITT *enters, relaxed, a little drunk, happy.)*

HAZLITT: Evening, Blue.

BLUE: Why Lieutenant. *(Big smile)* Again?

HAZLITT: Yes, ma'am.

*(*BLUE *rises and they stare at one another. Then they kiss.)*

BLUE: You better be careful, Lieutenant, we got a serious case here of me getting swept off my feet.

HAZLITT: Just so long as I'm doin' the sweepin,' ma'am.

BLUE: Charm, charm, charm. Y'all from the south?

HAZLITT: Southern California.

BLUE: Now that I didn't know.

HAZLITT: You been to L A?

BLUE: Of course.

HAZLITT: I'm from L A. Well the Valley. Tarzana.

BLUE: Tarzana... *(She smiles, little laugh.)*

HAZLITT: Named after Tarzan.

BLUE: I know. So when did this...tranny chasing start?

HAZLITT: You getting changed or what?

BLUE: You in a hurry?

HAZLITT: Big hurry. Big operation coming up. Tonight's sort of a send-off.

BLUE: *(Suddenly concerned)* Really?

HAZLITT: Don't worry. It's nothing dangerous. Nothing inordinately so.

BLUE: Nuthin' wrong with inordinate, but I'm glad it's not dangerous. *(Disappears behind screen to change)* So how did I get to be so lucky?

HAZLITT: I don't know. I used to go into town. With my friends. In high school. We'd go to *La Cage* on Cienega. There was a drag— *(Correcting himself)* An *actress* there I liked. Her name was Sheryl. We used to go out.

BLUE: *(Emerging in a stunning blue dress)* I bet you were something in high school.

HAZLITT: Jeez... Pimples, pot belly, pickin' my nose all the time. I was a mess. But she... She treated me like I was a Prince.

BLUE: *(Putting her arms around his neck)* Hmmm... Can't be a Princess without a Prince. So what happened to that pot-belly? I bet it was cute.

HAZLITT: (*Thwacking his tight stomach*) This? This is the Corps. Like everything else good in my life. Except... Well, except you.

BLUE: Hmmm... And whoever comes next.

HAZLITT: Now, you gonna get jealous of the future?

BLUE: A lady's never jealous. She only *acts* jealous. To get her way.

HAZLITT: Blue, you gonna get your way whether you want it or not.

BLUE: You are one crazy marine.

HAZLITT: And you're just the girl for me.

(*They kiss.* HAZLITT *is ready for more.*)

BLUE: Easy, Tiger. I wanna show you off first.

HAZLITT: Feeling's mutual, sweetie.

(*Blackout*)

Scene 5

(*Shift to...* DAME *is under a barracks lamp light, pacing. It is late at night.* HAZLITT *enters, not drunk, but relaxed.*)

HAZLITT: Hey, Dame.

DAME: Hazlitt. You ok?

HAZLITT: Yeah, how you?

DAME: Where you been?

HAZLITT: (*Irked*) Who's asking?

DAME: (*Starting to leave*) Forget it.

HAZLITT: (*Annoyed that he annoyed her*) Shit...Dame.

DAME: (*Stopping*) We got the green light. We're on tomorrow.

HAZLITT: (*This is sobering news*) Oh... Oh, cool.

DAME: Sooner than expected.

HAZLITT: Yeah.

DAME: But good news.

HAZLITT: Yeah.

DAME: It's a jump. Combat jump.

(HAZLITT *only looks at* DAME. *Beat)*

DAME: *(Leaving)* Good night.

HAZLITT: *(Distracted)* Yeah, right...

(DAME *stops, looks at* HAZLITT.)

HAZLITT: I mean, good night.

(HAZLITT *exits.* COLONEL *emerges from the shadows, a cigarette in his lips.* DAME *looks at him—she knew he was there.* COLONEL *holds her stare and crushes out his cigarette. She understands. She exits. Shift to...)*

Scene 6

(The interior of a plane. But really just a bare stage with a fire door exposed, long bench against the back wall. BRAVER *and* SOMERS, *two enlisted men, suited up for a jump—the full rig.* HAZLITT *and* DAME *are suiting up.* BRAVER *and* SOMERS *are about what we expect, real career grunt types,* BRAVER *perhaps a little more so than* SOMERS. COLONEL *in fatigues giving them the final what's-up. Aircraft sounds. All shout above sounds.)*

COLONEL: You're a small unit. Two officers, two men. So there won't be any shortage of leadership. Dame knows what to do. She's in charge.

HAZLITT: *(Confused, he was supposed to be in charge)* Sir?

COLONEL: Yes.

(Pause. They regard one another. HAZLITT *would never say anything in front of the men.)*

HAZLITT: Nothing.

COLONEL: *(Continuing)* You have three objectives. Dame knows what they are. Something happens to Dame, get on the horn, we'll feed you targets as they come. The important thing is to stay intact, complete all three, and come out of it. There's no surrender. Iraqis'd cut off your limbs then rape the rest.

DAME: Sir?

COLONEL: Yes, Dame.

DAME: Pilot's not Davenport. *(She's concerned but would never show it.)*

COLONEL: No.

DAME: New guy?

COLONEL: Good guy.

DAME: New?

COLONEL: *(Setting her straight)* There's only two words between you and the pilot. *(He points at the light by the door, which is dark.)* Red—stand-by. Green—go. He knows what he's doing.

DAME: New guy?

COLONEL: Anything else?

HAZLITT: How do we get away?

COLONEL: Dame knows. *(To all of them)* You're a small group. Economy. The best policy. Slip in, slip out, do some good and move on. Clean as a whistle. Fewer men, fewer fuck-ups. Everyone comes home safe. Democracy succeeds. Dame knows what to do. *(Shouting to cockpit)* All right, Hollister! Crank her up! *(Thunderous noise as engines start)* Noisy plane, silent warriors. Get some!

MEN: Arrugah!

(COLONEL *exits door. Door slams. Plane lurches, a big
lurch. Everyone shifts, but no one loses his balance.* DAME
looks at HAZLITT.)

DAME: *(Referring to the pilot)* New guy.

(Blackout)

Scene 7

(Spot on BLUE—*dressed in feathered costume and playing a
huge conga. We're in the Blue Parrot.* COLONEL *sits at table
in spot formerly occupied by* HAZLITT.)

(Song: Tarzana)

BLUE: *(Singing)*
Tarzana, I love ya.
Hot as hot as hot can be.
Your valley blossoms become ya
And the sun heats up and the boys grow up and they
make me shout out

Tarzana, I love ya
Hot as hot as hot can be
Your steamy sidewalks become ya
And the clouds role in, Santa Ana Winds blows in and
they proove to me that

Tarzana—

*(Police whistles—loud and obnoxious, obviously not part
of the number.* BLUE *stops singing.* COLONEL *stands up,
speaks to the crowd.)*

COLONEL: Sorry, folks. Show's over. Time to go home.

(We hear groans. BLUE *looks furious.)*

COLONEL: Hey, I'm not Shore Patrol. You can leave now, friendly like, or I call in the S Ps. *(More groans.)* Hey, I got the C I A on speed dial! *Vamanos!*

(Argument between COLONEL *and soldiers continues— ornery, drunks all of them—as the light fades.)*

VOICE: Fuck you, Colonel.

COLONEL: Hey sailor, get your fat butt back to your destroyer.

VOICE: Suck my fat butt, bitch!

COLONEL: You noisy piece of shit, I'll kick your arrogant ass!

Scene 8

(Shift to her dressing room immediately following. BLUE *enters and throws down her wig. She is furious.* DINAH BLUE *is a formidable character, as her songs and her relationship with* HAZLITT *should demonstrate. She is over six foot, in excellent health and stunning in her get-up. She has been through much and will live through more. The* COLONEL's *interruption of her act she sees only as the next in a lifetime of challenges. She actually has a fair amount of experience handling men like the* COLONEL. COLONEL *enters. She looks at him. Whatever the individual dynamics of the scene, it should be clear that these two understand and have a lot more sympathy for one another than might be expected.)*

BLUE: Well, Colonel. How can I help you?

COLONEL: I'm shutting you down.

BLUE: Why?

COLONEL: This is completely illegal. This entire operation.

BLUE: It's a nightclub, Colonel. Bird Colonels don't have nightclubs?

COLONEL: I already talked to your towel head owner. He's scared shitless.

BLUE: Thank you.

COLONEL: Sand niggers always bend when you press 'em.

(BLUE *and* COLONEL *regard one another. She tries a different tack, as she removes her make-up.*)

BLUE: Did you like the show?

COLONEL: Excuse me?

BLUE: Did you like the show?

COLONEL: I'm married.

BLUE: So am I.

COLONEL: Why do I have trouble believing that?

BLUE: To the stage. I've played everywhere: Kuwait, Qatar, Palermo, Nome, I even played in Bangladesh. All over the American Empire. You might even call me an empress. And do you know the one thing every place had in common.

COLONEL: An asshole like me who shut your tired ass down.

BLUE: An officer and a gentlemen, right?

COLONEL: *(He's heard enough)* Come on.

BLUE: Don't they train manners anymore? Whatever the Marine Corps was years ago—it had manners.

COLONEL: For drag queens?

BLUE: I'm not a drag queen. I'm an actress.

COLONEL: Listen Blue—

BLUE: Miss Blue.

COLONEL: Miss Blue. I went to college. In the eighties
I studied queer theory and the collapse of gender.
I know all about the fluidity of sexuality and the
performative nature of identity.

BLUE: *(Seductive)* My goodness.

COLONEL: I was also in a frat. So I know about that too.

BLUE: Personal experience?

COLONEL: As a matter of fact, yes.

BLUE: *(Actually surprised at his candor)* Bravo.

COLONEL: So I don't got no problem with you or your
kind. If this was the West Village I'd bring my wife
downtown for dinner and your show and we'd throw
fuckin' roses like you were the Divine Miss M.

BLUE: Your wife?

COLONEL: Or maybe a girl friend. But it's not. This is
Kuwait City. Every Network, Cable Network Wannabe
and on-line media freak is looking for a story and I
know you wanna be the next Lady Chablis. So rather
than wait around for that train wreck I'm shuttin'
you down. I've arranged evac for you and your…
costumes. Maybe it's time you tried Off-Broadway.

BLUE: Jealous, Colonel?

COLONEL: Lieutenant Hazlitt thinks there's a certain
latitude in an officer's comportment. There is. But not
this.

BLUE: Lieutenant Hazlitt is a gentleman.

COLONEL: Gentlemen follow the rules.

BLUE: They also show respect. There are any number
of ways you could have ended my act and still been a
nice guy. Where do you dig up these theatrics, some
Sam Shepherd play?

COLONEL: *(Mechanically)* I'm sorry. You're right.

(This surprises BLUE; *not just the comment but the efficiency of his retreat. She admires efficiency. She advances and spins.)*

BLUE: Can you unzip me?

COLONEL: Of course.

*(*COLONEL *does and* BLUE *steps behind screen to change.)*

BLUE: Where was this frat you belonged to?

*(*COLONEL *doesn't respond.)*

BLUE: Come on Colonel. You've got me. I surrender. Now be a nice guy about it, huh?

*(*COLONEL's *surprised by the casual turn the conversation's taken, but goes along.)*

COLONEL: Charlottesville, University of Virginia.

BLUE: My goodness, you *are* a drinker. Why the military? *(Pause)* Colonel?

COLONEL: I'm a Virginian. It's not considered a step down for us. Also, I wanted to get out.

BLUE: Of where?

COLONEL: Virginia.

BLUE: And your wife.

*(*COLONEL *sighs.)*

BLUE: Need a drink?

COLONEL: No, actually, I've had a few too many.

BLUE: You saw the show, didn't you?

COLONEL: Yeah.

BLUE: You really think I'm the Divine Miss M?

COLONEL: *(Smiling)* Better.

BLUE: Yeah?

COLONEL: Yeah. Because sober. I only saw her twice and she was loaded both times.

BLUE: Never go onstage drunk. Audience enjoys it too much. *(She emerges—stunning in a conservative blue dress.)* All set.

COLONEL: For what?

BLUE: That drink.

COLONEL: That is so not happening.

BLUE: I know a place.

COLONEL: A place?

BLUE: A place where journalists don't hang out.

(COLONEL smiles.)

COLONEL: Miss Blue—

BLUE: I know, you don't want me to get the wrong idea. Don't get nervous. I know queer and I know a man who just needs someone to talk to.

COLONEL: And I need someone to talk to?

BLUE: Birdie, you mind if I call you Birdie? Birdie, you could have sent shore patrol, you could have sent the Kuwaiti feds but you sent yourself. Now either you're more of a gentlemen than I thought or you wanted to see what was going on. I think, maybe, a little of both, *n'est-ce pas?*

COLONEL: O K.

BLUE: Journalists are afraid of air strikes and the locals. So they don't leave their hotels after dark. The town is ours.

(COLONEL is still reluctant.)

BLUE: You at least owe me a drink and making nice with me might help me leave quiet like. *Capiche?*

(COLONEL's still reluctant.)

BLUE: Who could I tell, Colonel? Who'd believe little ol' me?

(BLUE *extends her arm.* COLONEL *smiles. O K, why not? He takes her arm and they exit. Blackout. Aircraft sounds— loud.)*

Scene 9

(Lights up on Marines seated on long bench. Some rattling about indicated by actors. Red light snaps on.)

DAME: There's the red light. Suit up.

(They all stand and begin checking their gear.)

DAME: *(To* BRAVER*)* Hand me that radio, Happy.

(BRAVER *hands* DAME *the radio. She immediately begins smashing the radio on the deck, really fucking it up.)*

SOMERS: What the hell are you doing?

DAME: Nothing.

SOMERS: What are you—

DAME: *(Changing the subject, having finished her job on the radio)* Are you all set?

SOMERS: What are you—

DAME: I asked you a question.

SOMERS: Yes, sir. I am.

DAME: Good. *(To* BRAVER*)* Bad Boy, suit up. Hazlitt.

HAZLITT: What's up with the radio, Dame?

DAME: Nothing.

HAZLITT: What do you mean "nothing"?

DAME: Explanation's not going to bring it back.

HAZLITT: Goddammit, Dame

DAME: (*In his face*) No, goddammit, Hazlitt. Seen too many missions fucked up by radios. We have our orders.

HAZLITT: You're the only one who knows them.

DAME: Well then, you're just going to have to do what I say and make sure I don't get hurt, aren't ya? (*Red light flashes*) Here we go.

(*Crashing sounds—some kind of flak being fired at the aircraft.*)

DAME: Flak, stand by.

(*The plane rattles horribly, crashing about the sky both being shaken by close AA fire and swerving wildly to avoid it. Actors indicate these movements. All four remain surprisingly cool. They even look at each other coolly, checking out each other's cool. Their training really shows in this sequence. They've been trained not to waste energy on fear when they're helpless, when, if they die, there was nothing they could do to save themselves anyway. The green light comes on.*)

SOMERS: Green light.

(*All look at* DAME. *She doesn't move. Why not?*)

DAME: Too early.

(*The green light flashes quickly. They all stare at it.*)

DAME: Too early.

(*It continues to flash.*)

DAME: Way too early. No way we're over the D Z.

(*It flashes quickly. Plane begins to bank.*)

DAME: He's turning.

HAZLITT: Shit.

DAME: Go. Go. Go, go, go, go...

(One by one they go out the door until the cabin is empty. The green light flashes. Lights out. The green light flashes in the dark.)

Scene 10

(Shift to COLONEL *and* BLUE *sitting in a casual cafe—very comfortable. Easy music plays—Phil Collins.* COLONEL *is drunk, which doesn't mean much because he often is. Not sloppy, just relaxed, open and expansive. With men he would have to show off. With* BLUE, *as with a women, he can open up, confess some things, get it off his chest.)*

COLONEL: I'm no good at this, Blue. I never was. I joined up because I wanted to fight. I wanted *The Sands of Iwo Jima* and *The Longest Day*. And *Hell is for Heroes*. I wanted a real war like World War II or the Civil War even. Now it's all politics. "Don't Ask, Don't Tell," "Rules of Engagement," policy, policy, policy, till you wannna throw up.

BLUE: My favorite movies: *All About Eve* and *The Women*.

COLONEL: The Forties, goddammit, the Forties! We should have been born—no, we should have reached maturity in the Forties.

BLUE: *(Proposing a toast)* The Forties!

BLUE & COLONEL: The Forties.

(They knock them back. COLONEL *slams down his glass, upside down, and laughs. He's enjoying himself.)*

BLUE: *Sahara.*

COLONEL: *(Sighing)* Ah…*Sahara*. Now there's *the* desert war movie… Of all time

BLUE: Humphrey Bogart.

COLONEL: Bogart. That's what I wanted to be. Bogart with a Grant tank and Nazis for enemies. None of this concern about friendlies and collateral damage. A clean war. A war against Germans. Bogart.

BLUE: *Casablanca.*

(BLUE *and* COLONEL *both sigh.*)

COLONEL: It doesn't get any better than *Casablanca.*

BLUE: First time I saw Ingrid Bergman in that big hat, with that raincoat. I knew I wanted to be an actress.

COLONEL: Bergman? What about Bogart's hat? Bogart's coat? That gun of his. (*He laughs.*)

BLUE: Her lips. Her head thrown back.

COLONEL: "Whatever we lost, we got it back last night."

(*They sigh.* COLONEL *takes another drink.* BLUE *regards him.*)

COLONEL: My wife always says, "Why go to a movie when you can go to a party. There's always a party. Get something done. Never got anything done at a movie."

BLUE: Except enjoy yourself.

COLONEL: And now war movies are coming back. *Saving Private Ryan* and *Pearl Harbor* and...I mean, they suck but they're coming back.

(*Pause*)

BLUE: (*Fishing*) Your wife.

COLONEL: My wife. Well, a gentleman doesn't discuss his wife.

BLUE: Ambitious?

COLONEL: My wife? Like a great white shark.

BLUE: For you?

COLONEL: For me?

BLUE: For your career.

COLONEL: I don't even think she knows I'm in the Corps. Nah, she's got plenty of career on her hands. She's an attorney. Insurance. Corporate shit. Oil tanker spills a million tons in the Bay of Bengel and before the wild life of three oceans can choke to death on the shit she's on the plane. Ambulance chaser? My wife's a tanker chaser. She'd convince a jury the fish were going to die anyway, of congenital heart disease. She'd talk her way out of anything.

BLUE: And you?

COLONEL: Me? Lonely man, can't you tell?

BLUE: Cause you're talking to me?

COLONEL: Who the hell else am I going to talk to? Gotta be careful. People blab.

BLUE: And who'd believe me?

COLONEL: I thought... She and I thought, when we were young, Chief of Staff. Can't fight a real war, I can at least be Chief of Staff. One day.

BLUE: You're young.

COLONEL: But not headed in the right direction.

BLUE: I'd have thought you were a shoe in.

COLONEL: Nah, I'm not political. I don't have that kind of delicacy or that kind of smarts. I'm also not black or Chicano or Asian...

BLUE: You could be gay. That's the one minority anyone can sign up for.

COLONEL: Well, a young man will try anything, like I said. Nah, gay guys are just...too all over the place. I'm a one person guy. That's one thing women are, loyal. For the most part.

(BLUE *feels a subject change is in order.*)

BLUE: I was going to be a soap opera actress. That was my big ambition.

COLONEL: *(Appalled)* Soaps?

BLUE: Yeah, I wanted to act...a lot. "A lot" meaning "all the time." Quality, but also quantity. You see in the old days an actress would make four, five movies a year. Now it's one, one a year. I thought, "Film ain't for me. Not enough work." But T V wasn't for me either, apparently. I was too...quirky, too special, too something. So I went on the stage. That way I could perform every night. And it took me round the world. I might as well be Ingrid Bergman for the places I've seen, and the people I've met.

(They're quiet for moment, lost in thought.)

COLONEL: Hong Kong.

BLUE: Favorite place?

COLONEL: Yeah. Embassy security.

BLUE: Singapore.

COLONEL: *(Appalled)* Singapore

BLUE: Yeah, they looooved me in Singapore. The weather. *(She sighs—loved it.)* And the city. Like Epcot Center. Immaculate. I like immaculate. That's why I like military men, officers, they put a high premium on clean.

COLONEL: That we do.

BLUE: This mission those boys are on...

COLONEL: I'm not at liberty to discuss that.

BLUE: I just wanted to know...

COLONEL: Blue, you know better.

BLUE: Will I see Lieutenant Hazlitt? Again?

COLONEL: I thought you were a lady.

BLUE: I am.

COLONEL: Ladies don't discuss other gentlemen when they're on a date.

BLUE: Are we on a date?

COLONEL: Friends go on dates.

BLUE: Tell me something. Colonel. When you headed out tonight like John Wayne, did you see yourself ending the evening as Humphrey Bogart with me as Ingrid?

COLONEL: A good commander has back up plans, contingencies.

BLUE: Is that what I am? A contingency?

COLONEL: No, you're friend.

BLUE: A calculating man like you with friend like me?

COLONEL: Well, as you say, who you gonna tell?

BLUE: And who'd believe little ol' me?

COLONEL: Here's looking at you, kid.

(COLONEL *toasts* BLUE *and smiles.*)

Scene 11

(*Shift to* BRAVER *and* SOMERS *struggling in a field, getting oriented after their descent. It's dark. Damn dark.* DAME *enters, ready to go. Throughout the scene the Marines will look about, keeping watch, even when they're talking to each other.*)

DAME: How my Power Puff Girls?

(SOMERS *stares at her.*)

DAME: You O K?

SOMERS: Yeah, yeah fine.

DAME: *(To* BRAVER*)* Muscles?

BRAVER: Ship shape. I don't see anything.

SOMERS: What?

BRAVER: Where's our shit? Was supposed to be dropped this morning.

DAME: *(Looking out)* What's that mountain doing there?

BRAVER: *(Looking about him)* Nothing. There's supposed to be M16s, explosives, caps, cable…

(DAME *has produced a map, is studying it closely trying to get her bearings, cross checking it with G P S.* HAZLITT *stumbles on, clearly limping from a sprain.)*

HAZLITT: Dame.

SOMERS: You O K, Lieutenant?

HAZLITT: Yes. Perimeter!

(HAZLITT *gestures for* SOMERS *and* BRAVER *to maintain a lookout in all directions.)*

HAZLITT: Dame! This isn't right.

DAME: I know that.

HAZLITT: So?

DAME: *(Studying map)* We're wrong.

SOMERS: What?

DAME: This ain't our drop zone.

HAZLITT: Huh?

DAME: That's why you can't see anything. We missed our drop zone.

SOMERS: Oh, man.

DAME: Shut up, Dumpling. We're north, way north. We should be south of Dikip. We're north.

HAZLITT: That pilot.

DAME: *(Putting away map)* Yeah. Must have got scared by that flak and dumped us early. *(To* HAZLITT*)* New guy.

*(*HAZLITT *nods.)*

DAME: *(To* SOMERS *and* BRAVER*)* Ok. Gentlemen, we have about a thirty klick hike.

SOMERS: Shit!

DAME: *(Gesturing out)* That way.

SOMERS: *(Gesturing angrily as if talking to the chickenshit pilot)* Mother fucker, what the fuck!

HAZLITT: Load up, Somers.

DAME: We move, I mean *move*, we should make the r-vous.

SOMERS: What about our supplies?

DAME: Supplies made it. I know *that* pilot. Kurds will have them. No worries. All right, move out.

(Blackout)

Scene 12

(Lights back up low on the Marines moving through a field. They walk towards audience. Their motions are careful but confident. They have a long march ahead. Up to now they've been silent.)

SOMERS: Say Dame.

DAME: *(In whisper)* Fuck you, Squirrel.

SOMERS: Dame.

DAME: Keep your voice down, Rabbit.

SOMERS: *(In a whisper)* Why you always call me by a different name? *(To* BRAVER*)* She always calls me by a different name. Why is that?

DAME: *(Stops and stares at him)* Are you done? Are you?

SOMERS: Yeah.

DAME: Good.

(Gunfire. Tracers fill the air. Very sudden. There is a tremendous amount of noise. All four hit the deck, shoulder weapons and begin trying to find targets. Tracers are high.)

HAZLITT: I can't see anything.

BRAVER: Who's firing?

HAZLITT: Shit.

SOMERS: *(Overlapping others)* Doggone fuck me, shit. Fuck, fuck, fuck!

HAZLITT: What the hell is that?

DAME: Stay down.

(Tracers stop. Silence.)

BRAVER: It's stopped.

HAZLITT: Shit.

SOMERS: Who the fuck—

DAME: Stay down.

HAZLITT: What is happening?

SOMERS: *(Truly freaked)* Somebody tipped them off.

BRAVER: Who the hell—

SOMERS: Somebody tipped them off.

DAME: Shut up, both of youse.

HAZLITT: *(To* DAME*)* What do you think?

DAME: Not soldiers. Kids maybe. Someone playing with toys.

SOMERS: Toys. You call that toys? Motherfuckers with M16s are toys—

DAME: Will you shut up, Howser?

SOMERS: *(Losing it)* Cunt thinks it's toys.

DAME: Will you shut up?

SOMERS: Twat faced cunt, thinks it's—

(DAME *springs on top of* SOMERS *with her weapon drawn. She pins him down, knee on chest hand on his balls, and speaks directly into his face in a vicious whisper.)*

DAME: I *aksed* you, I *aksed* you a direct question, Dayton, will you shut up? *(She shoves her pistol in his mouth, fills his mouth with it, deep.)*

Will you? Simple answer: yes or no.

(SOMERS *nods his head "yes". She keeps pistol in his mouth. She looks. More tracers. This time the squad stays quiet. She keeps pistol in* SOMERS' *mouth. She looks. Even now she is on top of it all. Tracers stop. The rest in whisper.)*

DAME: Someone fucking around.

HAZLITT: 10-4 that.

DAME: Someone doesn't know how to handle a weapon. *(To* SOMERS*)* Listen to me, Alabama. You listening, Bama Boy?

(SOMERS *nods.)*

DAME: You're going to stay here and make a shit load of noise, like you did before. A lot of squawk. But you're going to stay here. Got it, Crawfish?

(SOMERS *nods. To* BRAVER*)*

DAME: Hummer, you'll go around left. Hazlitt, you'll go around right. I'll go with you, Hazlitt. *(To* BRAVER*)* Hummer, when you're in position lay down a shit load of fire but keep it low. You aim too high, you shoot me and I will shoot you. Copy?

BRAVER: 10-4, Dame.

DAME: Hazlitt, y'all set?

HAZLITT: Yeah.

DAME: *(To* SOMERS*)* Now, I'm taking your weapon, Joker. You don't need it. You're too cool for school. Just remember, you take off, you scram, I'll shoot you in the back. We're moving right, Hazlitt's covering them, I'm covering you. Copy, Jarhead?

(DAME *removes the gun from his mouth.* SOMERS *has shit his pants.)*

SOMERS: Yeah.

DAME: *(Squeezing his balls—tight)* Say, "Copy, Dame."

SOMERS: Copy, Dame.

DAME: "I like your tits, Dame."

SOMERS: I like your tits, Dame.

(DAME *releases* SOMERS *finally. She grabs his M14 and turns to* HAZLITT.*)*

DAME: O K, Hazlitt?

HAZLITT: Yo.

DAME: *(To* BRAVER*)* O K, Wiley?

BRAVER: Copy.

DAME: *(To* SOMERS*)* Freak, Drummer. *(Pointing pistol at him)* I said freak!

(SOMERS *starts screaming. He screams his head off.* DAME *and* HAZLITT *head out right.* BRAVER *heads out left.* SOMERS *is alone, screaming. Air fills with tracers. More noise than we've ever heard before.* SOMERS *looks panicked. He turns to flee but thinks better of it. He stops. And screams some more, with less conviction. He calms down but keeps screaming. Eventually he is very calm but keeps up his screaming; the tracers continue harmlessly overhead.*

*We hear some different sounds. Four deep plugs, then a large
explosion. Then two more plugs. Silence. No tracers. All
still.* SOMERS *stops screaming. Silence. Then five more deep
plugs. Silence. Long pause.* BRAVER *returns. He is breathing
hard, almost panting.* HAZLITT *and* DAME *come on from the
other direction. She is already studying a map.* HAZLITT *is
covered with blood.* SOMERS *checks them out, perplexed. He
wants to know what happened.)*

SOMERS: *(To* HAZLITT*)* You hit, Sir?

HAZLITT: Not my blood.

SOMERS: What happened?

BRAVER: Dame was right.

SOMERS: Right? 'Bout what?

BRAVER: They were kids.

SOMERS: Kids?

HAZLITT: Must have gotten the weapons from some
airdrop. Kids fucking around.

SOMERS: How'd you get blood on you?

BRAVER: They tried to surrender. Dame smoked them.

DAME: *(To* BRAVER*)* Fuck you, Bisquick.

HAZLITT: Their hands were up, Dame.

DAME: Fuck you, they were reaching for a grenade.

SOMERS: Kids?

DAME: Teenagers.

BRAVER: Little kids. No way teenagers.

SOMERS: *(Picking white stuff off of* HAZLITT*)* Shit. Look at
this shit.

DAME: *(Indicating direction)* We're this way.

SOMERS: *(Holding something white and bloody)* What the
fuck is this?

HAZLITT: What?

SOMERS: On your shirt.

BRAVER: Collar bone.

SOMERS: *(Throwing it away like it was a turd)* You're fucking kidding me.

BRAVER: Yeah, that's a collar bone. Piece of one.

SOMERS: I'm gonna be sick. *(He falls to his knees and starts to wretch.)*

DAME: *(To SOMERS)* Tracy, you heave I'll shoot you. Is that clear? Is it?

SOMERS: *(Choking it back)* Yes, sir.

DAME: Fucking childcare. I don't got time for this. Get your shit. We're this way.

BRAVER: *(To SOMERS)* You O K?

DAME: He's fine. Move out. Hazlitt.

HAZLITT: Take it easy, Dame.

DAME: Goddammit Hazlitt.

HAZLITT: Yeah, O K.

(HAZLITT exits. BRAVER follows. DAME looks at SOMERS. He looks terrified. She crosses to him and hands him his M14. He reaches for it but she won't let it go till she speaks her peace.)

DAME: Daisy, I just blew away two five year olds. I will not hesitate to blow your fucking head off if you can't square your ass away.

SOMERS: Sorry, Dame.

DAME: Fuck you apologizing like I'm your prom date. Grab your shit and haul ass, faggot.

(SOMERS does, quickly, and exits after HAZLITT and BRAVER. DAME looks after them, removes a large bayonet from her pack, then moves in their direction.)

Scene 13

(Shift to COLONEL *at his desk working at this laptop, focused.* BLUE *enters in a conservative lavender-blue lady's suit and scarf. He doesn't notice her.)*

BLUE: Good afternoon.

COLONEL: *(Looking up)* What the hell...

BLUE: The young man at the gate told me to give you this.

*(*BLUE *hands* COLONEL *an envelope stamped S S I A.)*

COLONEL: What...

BLUE: It's labeled S S I A. He said that's code for "Top Secret." And then he winked.

COLONEL: How the hell did you get in here?

BLUE: A lady knows how to get on a base.

COLONEL: No way.

BLUE: What?

COLONEL: No way S P at the gate thought you were a woman.

BLUE: Oh, he knew what was going on. There are many old boy networks, Colonel. And many overlaps.

COLONEL: *(Truly impressed)* Unbelievable. He gave you this?

*(*BLUE *nods and smiles.)*

COLONEL: Unbelievable.

BLUE: You better stop looking at my legs and open it Colonel.

COLONEL: *(Suddenly petulant)* I wasn't looking at your...

BLUE: It's highest priority.

(COLONEL *is truly amazed by* BLUE. *He shakes his head and smiles as he absently tears open the package. He reads. What he reads slowly settles in. He wanders towards his desk. He sits. He drops the document. His head falls into his hands. She has watched all this, intrigued.*)

BLUE: What is it, Colonel?

(COLONEL *ignores* BLUE. *He opens his phone and quickly dials. He's almost done dialing but suddenly he stops and shuts the phone. He looks at the phone. Opens it again. Takes a breath. Then shuts it. He throws the phone against the wall, violent.*)

BLUE: You sure you don't want to tell me?

(*Silence.* COLONEL *paces.*)

BLUE: Colonel.

(*Something in* BLUE's *tone gets* COLONEL's *attention.*)

BLUE: Looks like you can't tell anybody else.

(BLUE *stares at* COLONEL. *He takes a breath.*)

COLONEL: (*Almost blurting it out*) They're after the wrong guy.

BLUE: What?

COLONEL: They're going to shoot the wrong guy.

BLUE: Who is?

COLONEL: Your boy friend.

(*Now* BLUE *looks worried.*)

BLUE: I hate to put it this way, but does that matter?

COLONEL: Yes, it's a major fuck up.

BLUE: It's what?

COLONEL: It's a fuck up. I've screwed up. Shit! Shit! (*He beats up an innocent file cabinet. This is a wild moment of savagery.*)

BLUE: Easy. Easy, Tiger!

(COLONEL *is hunched on the floor.*)

BLUE: I can't help?

COLONEL: What?

BLUE: How can I help?

COLONEL: You know how to communicate by telepathy, soldier?

BLUE: No.

COLONEL: Voo Doo?

BLUE: Not yet.

COLONEL: You think this is a joke.

BLUE: No. You do.

(COLONEL *shakes his head. He doesn't begin to understand* BLUE.)

BLUE: You make a mistake you turn into Robert Duvall, method actor kicking file cabinets and swearing like a sailor. You screw up, someone dies. Do you even realize that? You act like it's just a bad break. Something to get dramatic about. A chance to trash an office. Then you'll apologize, eat shit with the General or the Admiral or whoever you suck up to and you'll go have a beer. Probably make you more popular with the brass. Make you human. A guy who makes mistakes. Am I right?

(COLONEL *turns away. He doesn't need this shit right now.*)

BLUE: Who's this *guy*?

COLONEL: What guy?

BLUE: (*Making fun of him*) This gook? This towel head? This sand nigger?

COLONEL: Head of the Peshmergas… Head of a faction of it.

BLUE: *(Again making fun of him)* Some wog.

(COLONEL *looks at her.*)

BLUE: What do you give that he dies?

COLONEL: Forget it.

BLUE: Tell me.

COLONEL: Nah.

BLUE: Tell me, Gerald.

(COLONEL *looks at her.*)

COLONEL: He dies, they die. Hazlitt, Dame, all of them.

BLUE: Why?

COLONEL: He's the wrong guy. We thought the Turks wanted him dead, but they don't. Neither do the peshis. No one's going to offer protection they kill him. I fucked up. I gave them the wrong guy.

BLUE: How did you do that?

COLONEL: Shit intell.

BLUE: *(Not understanding)* Shit and tell?

COLONEL: The names all look the same. His names' Fayet. The guy we want, wanted—he's dead now—is Fayed. Anyway, when they shoot *him* everyone in site is going to shoot *them*. It's just fucked up.

BLUE: *(Making an excuse for him)* You had shitty intell.

COLONEL: Nah, I did it myself.

BLUE: You did it yourself?

COLONEL: If I don't take the gig, if I didn't send out a squad Colonel Rodriguez would have. He had the bit in his teeth. He was all set to go, in like Flint with the General. He would have sent out a squad, gotten the kill and probably the star.

BLUE: But you had the intell...

COLONEL: Yeah… *(Punches file cabinet. Looks at her, embarrassed)* Hey, it's my cabinet. Rodriguez, fuckin'…

BLUE: Fuckin' what? Wetback?

COLONEL: Oh, frig you with your sensitivity training. That wetback means more to me than some tired faggot in ugly pumps. *(Gathers himself)* Sorry. Than some tired faggot in gorgeous pumps.

BLUE: You like my pumps?

COLONEL: I do. Actually.

BLUE: Thank you actually. *(Pause)* What are we going to do?

(COLONEL stares at BLUE— "we?")

COLONEL: Nothing.

BLUE: Nothing.

COLONEL: Can't send anyone after them, they're cut off. That's the thing with Spec Forc *(Pronounced "Fork")* —you go in as an air bubble—nothing in front of you, nothing behind. You lose communications, you are cut off. No way to get at them from Turkey.

BLUE: What about from here?

COLONEL: *(Sarcastic)* Yeah, you get a transport to fly north of Baghdad. Good luck.

BLUE: How's about on foot?

COLONEL: On the ground?

BLUE: Yes.

COLONEL: Impossible.

BLUE: *Kelly's Heroes.* Clint Eastwood went a hundred miles behind German lines to secure some gold.

COLONEL: No way.

BLUE: Someone could infiltrate. Go in disguise.

COLONEL: You know anyone around here who could pass for Arab?

BLUE: No one who could pass for an Arab *man*.

COLONEL: No way. *(He only stares at her realizing what she's suggesting.)* No way.

BLUE: Colonel…

COLONEL: You're serious? You'll get yourself killed.

BLUE: Would anybody notice?

COLONEL: Jesus.

BLUE: What do I tell them? If I get there?

COLONEL: Jesus.

BLUE: Colonel.

COLONEL: *(Annoyed with her)* Now you listen to me, I will lock you in the brig. I will. You wanna spend a week in the stockade?

BLUE: No, of course not.

COLONEL: Then butt out.

BLUE: What will you do?

COLONEL: Send someone. I'll figure it out.

BLUE: Who can you send? You can't trust anyone. You need someone expendable, disposable, someone who doesn't matter, someone wily enough to be Special Forces but not. Someone who never, in a million years, would spill to Colonel Rodriguez.

COLONEL: Leave me alone, this doesn't concern you.

BLUE: It doesn't? He's my boy friend.

COLONEL: I said butt out. I'm sorry but there's nothing you can do.

BLUE: Is there anything you can do?

COLONEL: I just need to…

BLUE: What?

COLONEL: Figure out how to get them to turn on their fucking radio.

Scene 14

(Shift to Marines standing in semi-light, dawn. HAZLITT *is downstage obviously talking to someone who is out front, unseen. Marines are upstage,* DAME *is furthest upstage, trying to disappear behind* BRAVER *and* SOMERS.*)*

HAZLITT: *(Out, as if someone has just finished talking to him)* O K, good, thank you. *(He crosses upstage to Marines and speaks to* DAME.*)* They say there are Fedayeen on the bridge. In a guard house. And a force on the other side of the river. No way can we take the bridge.

DAME: O K, then we blow it.

HAZLITT: We blow it?

DAME: Yes, orders are we can't take it, we blow it. Move on to our next objective. They have the explosives from the airdrop. We have cable, detonators and fuses. You'll go with them, take Braver. Keep an eye on the guard house. I'll take Somers and set the charges.

HAZLITT: Maybe I should take Somers.

DAME: He'll be fine. He just got shook up. He's our explosives guy. *(To* SOMERS*)* Somers, go with them and get the shit. Two backpacks. Two. I'll lag behind. When you got everything fall back with me and we'll check out the bridge.

SOMERS: Yes, sir.

HAZLITT: You called him, Somers.

DAME: All right, let's break it up before they get too
interested in me.

HAZLITT: *(Out to the guy he was speaking to before)* Hello.
Yes. We will blow up the bridge. *(Pause)* We must.

Scene 15

*(Shift to DAME and SOMERS clinging to different pilings of
a bridge—structural columns of the theatre itself. SOMERS
farther out with charges and explosives strapping them to
piling. DAME is struggling with wires. HAZLITT works his
way to DAME's piling as if through shallow water. This
scene is performed in low whispers as the enemy is overhead.
The work continues; it is agonizing hard work, lots of sweat.
Always they are snatching looks over their heads.)*

HAZLITT: We got a problem.

DAME: What?

HAZLITT: We got a problem.

DAME: Hajii?

HAZLITT: No.

DAME: What? *(To SOMERS, who has stopped wiring)* Keep
going. Just keep going. *(To HAZLITT)* What?

HAZLITT: Covering force.

DAME: Yeah.

HAZLITT: The Kurds.

DAME: *(Impatient)* What is it, Hazlitt?

HAZLITT: They say we killed their boys.

DAME: What?

HAZLITT: Little boys. They sent them off with guns to
hold a perimeter. Around the village.

DAME: I don't got time for this.

HAZLITT: They have Braver.

DAME: What?

HAZLITT: They started asking Braver questions about the little boys. Wanted to know where they were. Had he seen them? He said he had.

DAME: Are you kidding? Is this a joke? We're in the middle of wiring a bridge. They're supposed to be covering us—

HAZLITT: They're freaking out. I told Braver to shut his hole.

DAME: What are you doing here?

HAZLITT: I said I'd get our commanding officer.

DAME: Are you retarded? They think I'm a guy. I'm supposed to go back there and weasel us out of this? They'll toast us all. You fuck up!

HAZLITT: Goddammit, I didn't know what else to do. Do something. They'll shoot us if they find out what happened.

DAME: What the fuck were they sending kids out to hold a perimeter.

HAZLITT: They're short of men. They told the boys to shoot over our heads to scare us off, just in case we were Americans coming from the wrong direction. They told them to surrender if they were attacked. The Fedayeen don't shoot children.

DAME: Could this be more fucked up?

HAZLITT: Well…

DAME: Somers.

SOMERS: Yes, sir.

DAME: How you doing?

HAZLITT: O K.

DAME: *(As she speaks she removes bars from her collar)*
You're going back with Hazlitt. Hazlitt, Somers is a
Lieutenant. Our commanding officer. Pin the bars on
him. *(To* SOMERS*)* Tell them we saw the boys' bodies
when we came over the hill into the village. They were
already dead. When they ask why we didn't tell them
before say we didn't want to upset them. Tell them the
boys were both dead and their dicks were cut off and
shoved in their mouths. We didn't want them to know.
Say we're sorry.

(Silence. HAZLITT *and* SOMERS *just stare.)*

DAME: It's a tribal revenge thing. They'll understand.
Be reluctant to tell them. Make them drag it out of you.
Got it?

(Pause. SOMERS *just stares.)*

DAME: Got it?

SOMERS: Yeah.

HAZLITT: But that's not what they'll see when they find
the bodies.

DAME: Yes, it is. I took care of it. I thought we might
have this problem. *(To* SOMERS*)* Get going. I'll come in
right behind you with the wire. We blow this thing and
get the river between us and them. Move on to the next
objective.

(Blackout)

Scene 16

(Later. Lights up on BRAVER, HAZLITT, *and* SOMERS, *for
the first time sitting, almost relaxed. It is dark. There is no
fire but the feeling is they are bedding down, finally, around
a fire.)*

BRAVER: Some story, Somers.

SOMERS: Saved your ass. *(Pause)* It was Dame's idea.

BRAVER: I figured. You think she really did it?

SOMERS: What?

BRAVER: To the boys.

SOMERS: *(To his crotch)* I love you buddy. Yes, I do. *(To* BRAVER*)* I call him Sasquatch. *(Looking at* HAZLITT*)* You should have seen the Lieutenant Hazlitt's face when she came out with that one.

BRAVER: *(Deciding to lighten the mood)* Like he was gettin' a woody?

SOMERS: *(Laughing)* Like she was fuckin' Miss July doin' her centerfold.

(They laugh. HAZLITT *does not.)*

SOMERS: Say Lieutenant.

HAZLITT: Yeah?

SOMERS: When are you going to kill that bug that crawled up your ass?

(They laugh.)

HAZLITT: I like having things up my ass.

(They laugh.)

HAZLITT: Bug keeps me awake at night. Alert. Alive.

(They enjoy this. So does HAZLITT. *He knows he's a martinet, but he also knows he can show that knowledge and laugh with the men, at his own expense.)*

SOMERS: You think this mission's kosher?

HAZLITT: Kosher as in Jewish?

(They laugh.)

SOMERS: Do you think it's going to get some?

HAZLITT: You're Generation Kill, boy. You always get some.

BRAVER/SOMERS: Yeeeeaaaah!!!

HAZLITT: Tiger Tiger Tango!

BRAVER/SOMERS: T T T!

HAZLITT: Tiger Tiger Tango!

BRAVER/SOMERS: T T T!

HAZLITT: (Imitating the drill sergeant in *Full Metal Jacket*) "Show me your war face!"

(They growl with terrifying war faces.)

HAZLITT: "You don't scare me!"

(They get more intense.)

HAZLITT: "Work on it!"

(Now they're pumped up. BRAVER *and* SOMERS *sing "Burn, Motherfucker, Burn!" like raucous drunks.)*

HAZLITT: You already blew a fuckin' bridge, didn't ya?

SOMERS: That we did!

BRAVER: Sky high, sailor!

SOMERS: Rock and roll!

(BRAVER *and* SOMERS *high five and sing* Bombs Over Baghdad—*again like obnoxious drunks. Eventually they calm down. They want to talk, unwind.)*

BRAVER: But seriously, sir.

HAZLITT: What do you think, Somers?

SOMERS: I'm with Buttercup here.

HAZLITT: Yeah?

SOMERS: Yeah. I think it sucks.

HAZLITT: War?

SOMERS: Nah, peace! If we do land these bridges and end this fuck we'll be out of a job and back beggin' for checker at WalMart in '05.

BRAVER: Yep.

SOMERS: I think Bush Pére had it right: Long build up, long prep, long war. When it's done, it's done and I'm back with my wife. [That's a bad thing.]

BRAVER: Fuck that shit, man.

BRAVER & SOMERS: Arrugah.

SOMERS: I got a wife and kid. And I got them right where I want them. Home. I'm serious. Home. I can support them, they can do what they want and be proud of me. War ends. I'm unemployed and changing diapers; I've got one lady to fuck *(Meaning his wife, and that's bad)* and a kid I don't even know to take to the goddamn park.

BRAVER: Yeah.

SOMERS: Fuckin' Disneyland. Half mile away from my house. And I can't even afford that shit.

BRAVER: Yeah.

SOMERS: One hundred dollars a day. Disneyland. One hundred dollars a day! Here I'm king. Even in Beirut. I live like the Raj. You hear that, the Raj.

BRAVER: The Raj.

HAZLITT: What's the Raj?

SOMERS: *(To* BRAVER*)* Makepeace, it was Makepeace right?

BRAVER: Yeah, Makepeace.

SOMERS: Fuckin' Second Lieut. come through, assignment officer, co-ordinations in Lebanon. He had us read last summer. *Read.* He assigned us *Passage to India*. By Forster. *Had us read a book!*

BRAVER: Slowly like, man.

SOMERS: Yeah, chapter a week. Read and discuss. That's what he told us. We were the American Raj.

Places like Beirut, Guantanamo, Kuwait City, wherever Americans hold up overseas, we're like the British Empire. A place where a man like me can be a king, own property, live like an earl and build an Empire. The American Raj.

BRAVER: Fuckin' Philippines before Marcos.

SOMERS: Nam before Ho.

BRAVER: Hawaii before it became a state.

SOMERS: The Raj.

BRAVER: We'll remember, man.

SOMERS: Remember.

BRAVER: You married, sir?

HAZLITT: Nope.

SOMERS: You got something in K C?

HAZLITT: O K, Somers. *(Enough questions)* I like your Raj thing. This our India. I like that.

BRAVER: Friggin' Makepeace.

SOMERS: Frig yeah.

HAZLITT: What happened to him?

SOMERS: Stepped on a landmine.

BRAVER: The professor.

(He makes an explosion gesture to show what happened to Makepeace.)

SOMERS: Bye, bye Miss American Pie

(DAME enters. She isn't relaxed but she's shed some gear.)

DAME: You guys going to stay up all night?

HAZLITT: You better knock off, men.

DAME: *(During the following she's talking to SOMERS but looking at HAZLITT; she's talking about HAZLITT.)* Passage to India, Somersby.

SOMERS: Yeah.

DAME: Written by a man named Forster.

SOMERS: Yeah, E M, man, I remember that.

DAME: Faggot. Fantasies of empire in his head, but at home, he did with boys.

SOMERS: Yeah. Faggot, huh?

BRAVER: Yeah. Makepeace never told us that.

SOMERS: *(Playing)* Braver here is faggot.

BRAVER: *(Playing back, not at all offended)* Shut your hole, Shirley!

SOMERS: Or you like to be called queer now, right?

BRAVER: Yeah, Metrosexual. Easier to get a date.

SOMERS: Women lookin' for a ring…

BRAVER & SOMERS: Men just lookin' to nut.

(BRAVER and SOMERS wrestle. And laugh wildly,)

HAZLITT: All right, knock it off you two.

(BRAVER and SOMERS crawl off towards their tents, laughing. We really should have no sense that these two are actually gay.)

DAME: Not much point in dousing lights if you're going to let them make so much noise.

HAZLITT: You're right, Lieut.

DAME: Fuck you I'm right. What's your problem, Hazzle? Think I'm looking for a ring?

HAZLITT: Actually I don't.

DAME: "Actually I don't." Where did you learn to talk like that? The Colonel?

HAZLITT: Watching old movies.

DAME: Fuck you.

HAZLITT: On television. When I was a kid.

DAME: You're still a kid.

HAZLITT: Yeah, that's why I'm here. The adventure.

DAME: I wish you'd shut up about that. The adventure. You and the Colonel. The adventure. It's a job, Hassle. It just *is*. Like working for Walmart or Costco or BestBuy. You restock, you open up, you ring up, then you close out your register. It's employment.

HAZLITT: So why don't you work for Costco?

DAME: They wouldn't hire me. *(Silence)* You think I'm pretty?

(Pause. HAZLITT can't believe the question, that she's asking it, here.)

HAZLITT: What?

DAME: *(Confrontational)* You heard me.

(HAZLITT exhales, can't believe this is happening but willing to go along.)

HAZLITT: You know I do.

DAME: Then why did you stop fucking me?

(HAZLITT takes a deep breath. Exhale. Maybe he's wrong, maybe DAME just wants to fight.)

DAME: What does that mean?

(HAZLITT rubs his face. Looks at DAME. He stands. He moves towards her. Then away)

DAME: What?

(HAZLITT doesn't respond.)

DAME: *(Showing just how stressed she is)* Do you…

HAZLITT: What?

DAME: Do you have any idea…

HAZLITT: What?

DAME: What it's like dealing with these…situations?

HAZLITT: No, actually, I don't. *(He looks away.)* That's why you're in charge.

DAME: Forget it.

(HAZLITT decides his first impulse was right. DAME's lonely. So is he. And they're both freaked out, tense. He crosses to her. Touches her face. She likes it.)

DAME: Show us your tits.

(He takes his shirt off as she rubs his chest. He is topless. She rubs it some more, then kisses it. He lets her. We hear SOMERS and BRAVER giggling off.)

HAZLITT: Braver, Somers. Go to sleep!

SOMERS: Will you tuck us in mommy?

(More giggling)

DAME: I'll toss a grenade over there!

(Quiet. DAME goes back to HAZLITT's chest, she is unbuckling his fatigues. Blackout)

Scene 17

(Later. Moonlight. HAZLITT in his skivvies, DAME getting dressed. She's finished and ready to move on.)

HAZLITT: What's with the names?

DAME: Huh?

HAZLITT: Calling everyone by a different name.

DAME: You're always Hazlitt.

HAZLITT: Ok, the men.

DAME: They're men. They're not officers. They don't need names.

HAZLITT: What's up with that shit?

DAME: *(Losing it, throwing down her gear, in his face all of sudden)* Fuck you, Hazlitt. What do you want? A heart to heart? You fuck me you think you've earned some intimacy and shit?

HAZLITT: Christ, Dame.

DAME: I'll tell you "what's with the names". Maybe I don't want something I might have to kill or torture... Maybe I don't want it to have a name. It's bad enough they have a face. But a name, that really fucks it up. Takes the pleasure out of it. Is that the answer you wanted? Or how about my fucked up childhood explanation. This is for real, it is: I used to pull animals apart, slowly—like tics and flies and spiders at first, just shit that annoyed me, as punishment. Let it wobble around with one leg for a while. And eventually cats and little dogs and once this fucking rooster that our neighbors owned and that screamed its head off every morning at 500 A M. They didn't have names. Or at least not names I knew. Bad enough they had a face. But names. Names are personalities, attributes. *(Pause)* You ever twist the front leg off a kitten, you ever do that?

HAZLITT: O K—

DAME: Or a dog as it howls. Or once, this is sick, and definitely *entre nous*, my friend Cathy got pregnant and she was fourteen and I convinced her I could take care of it so—

HAZLITT: Jesus. Yes, fine, forget it.

DAME: *(Back in control)* Sorry. I'm bitter. Obviously.

HAZLITT: I don't get it.

DAME: What—

HAZLITT: You're so...

DAME: Yeah, yeah, O K. Yeah, I know. Living in the past. Fucked up childhood, so now I'm fucking up my life, I got it. Sorry. I am. I'm truly sorry. No. I am. Sorry to…drag you into it. Into my shit… *(Opening up)* I got a name. It's Shirley. How about that? Shirley.

HAZLITT: Look.

DAME: No, I…

HAZLITT: No, just stop, please…

DAME: What?

HAZLITT: It's just…

DAME: What? I want to know.

HAZLITT: This is worse.

DAME: What?

HAZLITT: You… Opening up… It's…

DAME: What?

HAZLITT: It's fucking awful. I feel like you're…licking my hand or something. Just…stop. O K?

DAME: Yeah. *(She throws up her hands—what a fucked up conversation. She's frustrated, makes some noises. She returns to her gear.)*

HAZLITT: *(Amused)* Shirley?

DAME: Look don't start.

HAZLITT: Shirley?

Scene 18

(Shift to COLONEL *pacing. He looks worried. It's as if he feels if he thought about something other than the operation it would curse the operation. His cell rings. He grabs at it quickly.)*

COLONEL: Yes. Yes, it's me. YHQBR14. Yes. Ok. Put it through. *(He waits. Impatient. Hopeful. Suddenly disappointment crosses his face. Not the call he wanted.)* Hey. How are you? Good. Good. It's good to hear from you. Busy. Very busy. Here? You're kidding. When? Why? I mean, it's a war zone. Is it business? You did? How? You're kidding, you're representing those grifters? *(Smiles)* Carol, you always get the acorns, don't you? No, I'm impressed. Always have been. No, no, come. Come. I want to see you. Yes. The weather? Hot. It's hot. *(Sarcastic)* It's a desert, Carol.

Scene 19

(Shift to HAZLITT *once again standing D C talking to someone—this time the someone is right of the audience, obscured by a curtained area audience right. The others huddle upstage,* DAME *again trying to disappear, not attract any attention.)*

HAZLITT: *(Out)* Who? Yes. I understand. I do. Yes.

*(*HAZLITT *crosses upstage to the huddle. He talks to* DAME. *Gesturing towards the man he was talking to)*

HAZLITT: O K, that's him. That's Fayet.

*(*DAME *sneaks a look.)*

HAZLITT: He says there's someone here to meet us.

DAME: *(Can't believe it)* What?

HAZLITT: He says someone has come to meet us. Got here yesterday.

DAME: Who?

HAZLITT: "One of ours." That's all he said.

DAME: One of ours? One of ours? No way one of ours got here before us. No fuckin' way, Hazlitt. Dropped in before us? No way.

HAZLITT: Not from the north. From the south.

DAME: *(Really can't believe it)* What?

HAZLITT: They came from the south. In the back of a truck.

(DAME stares at HAZLITT—her look says, "What the hell is going on?")

HAZLITT: Where is everyone?

DAME: What?

HAZLITT: Well, Fayet's all alone. Except for this person he's brought with him. He should be surrounded by peshis.

DAME: I set it up that way.

HAZLITT: *(Confused)* What?

DAME: Tell Fayet to send this person. Tell him to get this person quickly.

(HAZLITT crosses D C.)

HAZLITT: *(Out)* Send them. Send them here. Yes.

(We hear the sound of feet receding on gravel—the man is walking away. HAZLITT returns to DAME.)

HAZLITT: So how do you know he's alone?

DAME: What?

HAZLITT: How do you know Fayet came alone?

DAME: I asked him to. He trusts me.

HAZLITT: How?

(DAME looks at HAZLITT.)

HAZLITT: How did you ask him without a fukin' radio?

(DAME only looks at HAZLITT. We hear the sound of someone approaching on gravel. They all look. The sound stops.)

HAZLITT: *(Out)* Who are you?

(A person in full burka enters from the curtained area and crosses to HAZLITT. *Person removes the shador, revealing face. It's* BLUE. *All are stunned. They respond as they would normally to anything surprising; they all raise their weapons at the ready, shouting, frantic, on the verge of firing.)*

HAZLITT: *(To the men)* Whoa, whoa... Easy. Easy... This is an agent. Agent. Male agent. Man. Our man.

(The weapons go down. DAME *steps forward.)*

BLUE: *(Recovering)* Thank you, Tom.

HAZLITT: *(Speechless, not angry)* Wha... What the hell are you doing here?

DAME: *(To* HAZLITT*)* You know this person?

HAZLITT: Yeah...from K C.

DAME: *(Shaking her head)* Now I have seen everything.

BLUE: Are you all right?

HAZLITT: Stop. Not now, O K?

DAME: This takes the cake.

BLUE: *(To* DAME*)* Jessup. Colonel Jessup. He said...he said, "Turn on your radio."

*(*DAME *looks at* BRAVER. *She looks back at* BLUE.*)*

SOMERS: Dame smashed it.

BLUE: What?

HAZLITT: Lieutenant Anderson destroyed it. On the plane.

BLUE: Oh.

DAME: What's your fucking message?

BLUE: The man you were supposed to kill.

DAME: Yeah?

BLUE: Don't. He's the wrong guy. Bad intell. Kill him and you'll never get out of here. He's the wrong guy.

HAZLITT: He is?

DAME: Now what made the Colonel think I'd believe *you?*

HAZLITT: He didn't. He knew I would.

DAME: This is… This is right out of *The Twilight Zone*, not the old ones, the new shitty ones on Cable. *(To* BLUE*)* I mean, you're like a bad episode of *Cops*.

*(*DAME *strides away. She is frustrated, pissed off.* HAZLITT *crosses to her.)*

HAZLITT: So?

DAME: So what?

HAZLITT: So we shoot Fayet, we don't get out of here. Situation's changed.

DAME: How so?

HAZLITT: He's the wrong guy.

DAME: You know, I always knew this about Colonel Jessup. Someone once told me he was being groomed for General Staff. Big time. Then I met him… and here's this moony dreamer, sneakin' off to Bargain Matinees and always talking about Tom Clancy shit he's read. I humped my ass through four years of Anapolis learning about "I Transits" and C P Y I ops and he gets away with mucho time off because he's fun at a party. He probably, in some sick way, thought he was getting a piece of Robert Ludlam with this one.

BLUE: You're a very high strung young lady.

HAZLITT: Let's just go. Before he comes back. Let's just split.

BLUE: Colonel said you could bypass him and move on to your next objective.

DAME: You know what that is?

BLUE: What what is?

DAME: My next objective.

BLUE: No. Colonel said you did.

DAME: Oh, yeah, I do.

SOMERS: Let's split, man.

BRAVER: *(To DAME)* Should we confirm, Lieutenant?

DAME: No.

HAZLITT: Confirm what?

BRAVER: Lieutenant, should we confirm that order?

HAZLITT: How can you—

DAME: *(To BRAVER)* Shut up.

BRAVER: Lieutenant.

DAME: *(Seeing something)* Too late.

(We hear crunching sounds approaching from off. The man is approaching. They all look out.)

DAME: Too late.

HAZLITT: Let me talk to him.

(The crunching sounds stop. They all look. DAME walks forward, not at all trying to mask the fact that she's a woman.)

DAME: *(Friendly to man off)* Hey, hey, Khimosabe. Fayet baby!

(DAME points her gun off and unloads her clip into the man. We hear a body fall off. The men are shocked. They stare at body, almost as if they expect it to do something. DAME calmly replaces her clip with a loaded one. HAZLITT turns and stares at her, as if he already knew the answer to his question.)

HAZLITT: What's the next objective?

DAME: Shoot you in the fucking head!

(And DAME *is on* HAZLITT—*forcing him down, pinioning his weapon arm to the ground with her knee and forcing her automatic to his temple, his head in the dust.* SOMERS *calmly levels his rifle at* DAME's *head.)*

BRAVER: Jesus, Dame.

SOMERS: Lieutenant.

DAME: My third objective.

BLUE: What are you doing?

DAME: Jessup said if it ever got out that a Quantico Boy had shacked up with some faggot tranny freak it would be the end of the Corps. So I was to blow the bridge, ice Fayet here and then waste you. Mission accomplished.

BRAVER: Jesus.

SOMERS: Lieutenant.

DAME: What is it, Somers?

SOMERS: Eject your cartridge and put down that weapon.

DAME: Eat me, Somers.

SOMERS: I *will* shoot you, Lieutenant.

DAME: Eat me. You won't shoot until I shoot. R O E.

SOMERS: Then you better shoot quick Lieutenant because I will fire on three. One, two—

*(*DAME *stands, raises her weapon arm away from* HAZLITT *and moves away.)*

SOMERS: Lieutenant, eject—

DAME: Yeah, yeah, yeah… *(She throws her gun down.)*

BLUE: Were those your orders?

*(*DAME *only laughs.)*

BLUE: Were they?

DAME: Shoulder your weapon, Somers. It's over.

SOMERS: Lieutenant, raise your hands over your head—

DAME: Gimme a break, Sunshine, I nurse maid you through this entire operation. You would be paint back in Turkey now if it weren't for me.

BLUE: Were those your orders?

(*Always the unexpected,* DAME *begins undressing, shedding her belts, then her fatigues, soon she will be in skivvies.*)

DAME: (*To* BLUE) I'll need that rig.

BLUE: What rig?

DAME: That rig. Your shador or whatever you call it.

BLUE: What are you talking about?

DAME: We're going to have to hump it on foot to the nearest Coalition Unit. I'll pass faster in that than this. You can wear my fatigues.

BLUE: I got this far in this rig, I can make it back.

DAME: Yeah, but I can't. Not in this fucking country. Come on.

BLUE: You haven't answered my question.

DAME: And I'm not going to. (*To* BRAVER) Braver, get on the horn. Tell evac we won't need transport. We're going south.

(BRAVER *produces a small radio and begins punching numbers to activate it.* HAZLITT *can only shake his head.*)

BLUE: (*Indicating the dead body*) What about him?

DAME: Fuck him. Colonel thought we'd be meeting him with his posse. I knew we should meet him alone. In case something like this came up. So I wired ahead. They won't find him till tonight. By then we'll be smoke. I'll prep him so they think it was another tribe. (*She stares at* BLUE, *impatient.*) I know you hate me but do me the fucking favor of being the first goddamn person on this operation to quickly obey my orders. I do fucking know what I'm doing. I think that's the one thing we can all agree on.

(BLUE *begins to shed her burka. She is wearing fatigues underneath. They all look mildly surprised.*)

BLUE: *(Explaining)* In the theatre, it's called under-dressing.

(Blackout)

Scene 20

(Spot on BLUE, *still in her fatigues and wig. She will shed her wig and eyelashes as the song precedes.)*

(Song: "Goodbye")

BLUE: *(Singing)*
Goodbye to all that, goodbye to the war.
Goodbye to passions, explosions, mutations, and what's more:
Goodbye to the lies, goodbye to disguise,
Goodbye to Colonels, Lieutenants, Captains, goodbye to the guys.

Oh, I've seen so much, in the midst of gods.
I've seen it all: geniuses and clods.
So when I came, I knew a lot.
Now I know more: maybe not.

(During this next part she shoves her wig and make-up items into a canvas duffel. By the end of the song she resembles just another soldier ready to ship out.)

Goodbye to the tour, goodbye to the cheers.
Goodbye to the men, to the love and goodbye to the tears.
Goodbye to the dreams, farewell to the schemes.

In the midst of a war, there's no time for a whore who
is not what she seems.

Oh, I've seen so much, in the midst of gods.
I've seen it all: geniuses and clods.
So when I came, I knew a lot.
Now I know more: maybe not.

(Fade to black)

Scene 21

*(In the darkness we hear the sounds of aircraft taking off.
Lights up on* BLUE, *with her duffel, facing the* COLONEL.
*They stand in an air base waiting room. We hear occasional
announcements.)*

BLUE: You knew I'd go. You hoped I would. That I'd
work my little network to save your little network.
I was your B-plan. In case your primary didn't get
through. Right? Just say it, Gerald: You needed a
contingency and you read my file, before you even
came to the Blue Parrot. And even if this little parrot
squawked who'd listen?

*(*COLONEL *is silent.)*

BLUE: What price glory, eh Colonel? The one thing I
didn't like.

COLONEL: What?

BLUE: That man. He got killed. He got killed anyway.

COLONEL: She was hedging her bets. She made
arrangements to carry out her orders in spite of
changes. It's what she's trained to do.

BLUE: But that man. He was innocent. Well, I don't
know about innocent… At least he was on our side.

COLONEL: According to latest intell.

BLUE: So that's it then? She got away with killing him, no matter what side, so it's ok?

COLONEL: That's how she'll go one day. She knows that.

BLUE: And what does that say about the cause?

COLONEL: What cause?

BLUE: The coalition cause. The American cause. Our cause.

COLONEL: We're employees. We sell things. We perform tasks. You don't ask an employee at Costco about his cause. You ask him how much toilet paper in bulk he sold. Lieutenant Anderson sells a lot of toilet paper. She's an excellent employee.

BLUE: And Lieutenant Hazlitt?

COLONEL: Maybe one day.

BLUE: One day what?

COLONEL: Maybe one day he'll sell more toilet paper.

BLUE: You know my next question.

COLONEL: And you know my answer.

BLUE: You can tell me. Who could I tell? Who would believe me?

COLONEL: You would.

BLUE: And that matters? *(Pause)* Was it in her orders to shoot Tom?

(Silence. BLUE hands COLONEL some paper work. He looks at her for a minute. He knows what he's holding. Finally, he looks at it.)

COLONEL: Los Angeles?

BLUE: Yep.

COLONEL: No soldiers in L A…to entertain. Well, no warriors.

BLUE: I don't think I'm cut out to be a camp follower.

COLONEL: I thought that was your calling?

BLUE: It's a young woman's job.

COLONEL: You're young.

BLUE: I've gotten conservative in my middle age. I disapprove of things. An entertainer makes choices about whom she entertains.

COLONEL: The yobs at home contribute to this mess as much as the guy who pulls the trigger.

BLUE: Yeah, but they don't pull the trigger. And some of them hate it.

COLONEL: It's easy to hate it in L A. Then you climb into your S U V and bitch about gas prices.

BLUE: So, I'll ride a bike.

(COLONEL *signs the papers. Hands them to* BLUE.)

COLONEL: Soaps?

BLUE: Maybe. Your wife?

COLONEL: Maybe.

(BLUE *picks up her duffel and starts to leave.*)

COLONEL: Blue.

BLUE: Yeah, Colonel.

COLONEL: Get some.

(BLUE *smiles.*)

BLUE: Break a leg.

(BLUE *exits.* COLONEL *smiles. He opens his phone and dials. He waits.*)

COLONEL: *(Into phone)* Hey. Well, I'm here, where the hell are you? What? Officer's lounge? In this dump? I didn't even know we had one. *(He is exiting.)* Carol, are you drunk?

(Lights fade.)

Scene 22

(Aircraft noises become louder. Lights up on HAZLITT *and* BLUE. HAZLITT *also has a duffel. The noise is such they are obviously on the tarmac itself. They have to shout to be heard.)*

HAZLITT: Home.

BLUE: Tarzana?

HAZLITT: Well, Washington. Desk job. I'm not cut out for this.

BLUE: You're quitting?

HAZLITT: Not the military. It's me. It's where I belong. But I lack the combat thing. The Dame thing.

BLUE: The New Woman. I lack it too. I'm the Old Woman. Wise. World weary. Non-violent.

HAZLITT: Where you sitting? *(He grabs her ticket and looks at it.)* You've got shit connections. You're in steerage.

BLUE: This is steerage?

HAZLITT: It's practically a bench. Where they put the enlisted men. *(He picks up her duffel and throws it over his shoulder.)* Come on. You sit with me. I'll give you an upgrade.

(BLUE and HAZLITT exit like a couple of guys. A large aircraft flies by. The noise is almost deafening, that's how they like it in the Corps. Loud. Fade to black)

END OF PLAY